1 MONTH OF
FREE
READING

at
www.ForgottenBooks.com

By purchasing this book you are
eligible for one month membership to
ForgottenBooks.com, giving you
unlimited access to our entire
collection of over 1,000,000 titles via
our web site and mobile apps.

To claim your free month visit:
www.forgottenbooks.com/free866345

English
Français
Deutsche
Italiano
Español
Português

www.forgottenbooks.com

Mythology Photography **Fiction**
Fishing Christianity **Art** Cooking
Essays Buddhism Freemasonry
Medicine **Biology** Music **Ancient
Egypt** Evolution Carpentry Physics
Dance Geology **Mathematics** Fitness
Shakespeare **Folklore** Yoga Marketing
Confidence Immortality Biographies
Poetry **Psychology** Witchcraft
Electronics Chemistry History **Law**
Accounting **Philosophy** Anthropology
Alchemy Drama Quantum Mechanics
Atheism Sexual Health **Ancient History**
Entrepreneurship Languages Sport
Paleontology Needlework Islam
Metaphysics Investment Archaeology
Parenting Statistics Criminology
Motivational

SCIENTIFIC STOCK SPECULATION

By CHARLES H. DOW

With Introduction and Notes
By G. C. SELDEN

A condensed statement of the principles upon which
successful stock speculation must
be based.

The MAGAZINE of WALL STREET
NEW YORK

CONTENTS.

CONTENTS.

INTRODUCTION

By G. C. SELDEN

MR. CHARLES H. DOW, formerly the head of the Dow-Jones News Bureau, Wall Street's largest news gathering agency, had unusual opportunities for observing the methods of traders in stocks, both successful and unsuccessful. And it may be added that at the time of his death it was found that he had profited substantially by his accumulated knowledge.

About the year 1902 he wrote for the *Wall Street Journal* a series of articles on the science of stock speculation which attracted much attention. They were reprinted in book form, but the book has long been out of print. These articles are here reproduced just as he wrote them.

A good deal of water has flowed under the bridge since 1902, but there has been no change in the essential principles which Mr. Dow laid down. This is in itself a strong tribute to their permanent value, when we consider the great changes that have taken place not only in the stock market itself but in the country at large, in banking methods, in the promotion and sale of new securities, in the personnel of Wall Street and so on.

In 1902 the railroad stocks were the principal part of the market. They were the favorites not only with investors but with speculators also. The U. S. Steel Corporation had been organized the previous year, the stock had been well distributed to investors, and in 1904 it sold below $10 a share. Other industrials passed through a similar experience and were for the most part regarded questioningly.

This, it will be remembered, was before the heyday of Harriman. Even two years later, in 1904, Union Pacific sold at 71, and it was not until 1909 that its high price of 219 was reached. Only 4% dividends were paid on it in 1902.

The days of big speculation and wide price changes in industrial stocks had not then arrived. The few stocks which sold at very high prices were of an investment character and had an inactive market. The active speculation was in medium and low-priced issues.

It is important to bear these differences in mind in order to get the full grasp of Mr. Dow's idea. If he were writing today, he would not make any essential changes in the principles laid down; but he would probably modify some of his statements and would present a wider range of illustrations of the application of his methods to different classes of securities.

I have not been willing to tamper with a text so clear, succint and well worded, but have added some notes, in order to call attention to some of the more important changes in conditions and market customs which have taken place since Mr. Dow wrote.

There are many, of course, who will quarrel with the title of this book, "Scientific Stock Speculation," on the ground that speculation can never be reduced to a science. It is true that it cannot be reduced to a *mathematical* science, but it is certainly entitled to be called a science in the same sense that economics is a science.

Science in speculation must deal with tendencies rather than with exact mathematical conclusions. It is very noticeable that those who are most successful as investors for profit are usually of the type of the business man rather than the trained student of mathematics. The mathematician is always seeking some invariable rule or fundamental principle of fluctuations. This he cannot find. All speculative rules must be approximate. Any rule may be upset by the sudden development of new conditions.

To take as an example the old problem of the man rowing a boat directly across a river in a high wind: The mathematician, if given the rower's rate of speed, the rate of flow of the river, and the effect of the wind on the boat, can resolve these forces and show how far down the river the landing will be at the other side.

But to resolve the forces which control the price of a stock, a hundred different influences might have to be taken into account, some important and some slight, all varying constantly in the amount of their effect, and with the ever-recurring possibility of some new force appearing which would be temporarily more powerful than all the others put together.

Clearly this constitutes a problem beyond the reach of mathematics. Yet it is quite possible to estimate the importance of the principal elements in the situation; to make reasonable allowances for the possibility of some new factor entering in; to see in advance some of the changes which are impending; and to adjust the available capital to the character of the opportunity by means of the principle of averaging in some form, so that results are obtained which may properly be called scientific in a correct sense of that word.

Mr. Dow brings out very clearly the two ways in which the principle of averaging is employed in speculation:

(1) By buying small lots of a stock at fixed price intervals as it declines, and

(2) Taking small losses when wrong and calculating for a certain average of correctness; that is, for being right three times out of five, or four times out of seven.

While the two plans are diametrically opposite in practice, both are based on the idea of averaging. It is probably safe to say that nine out of ten successful speculators make use of this principle of averaging in some form.

The chapter on "The Recurrence of Crises" is, of course, intended merely as a brief sketch of the subject. It is evident that Mr. Dow had not devoted much attention to the study of trade cycles. In fact, most of the progress in making practical use of the idea of cycles has been made since he wrote.

Methods of trading which stand the test of twenty years without the necessity of any important revision necessarily command respect, and it is probably not too much to say that no one should begin his stock market experience without having absorbed, from some source or other, the ideas which Mr. Dow presents so briefly and clearly in this book.

CHAPTER I.

Scientific Speculation.

THE question whether there is such a thing as scientific speculation is often asked. Various answers of a somewhat affirmative character have been given but they have generally been hedged about with so many qualifications as to be nearly useless for practical purposes. The experiences of operators have, however, crystallized into some general rules worth heeding.

The maxim "buy cheap and sell dear" is as old as speculation itself, but it leaves unsolved the question of when a security or a commodity is cheap and when it is dear, and this is the vital point.

The elder Rothschilds are said to have acted on the principle that it was well to buy a property of known value when others wanted to sell and to sell when others wanted to buy. There is a great deal of sound wisdom in this. The public, as a whole, buys at the wrong time and sells at the wrong time. The reason is that markets

11

are made in part by manipulation and the public buys on manipulated advances and after they are well along. Hence it buys at the time when manipulators wish to sell and sells when manipulators wish to buy. (*See Note* 1.)

NOTE 1.—It is probable that Mr. Dow had in mind the manipulation of a single stock or group of stocks, rather than of the market as a whole. The whole market taken together is too big to be successfully handled by any manipulator or group of manipulators. This, in fact, grows less and less possible every year as the numbers of securities and of investors increase.

On the other hand, it is naturally in times when the public becomes enthusiastic that various manipulators are busy in different issues, so that near the climax of a big bull market manipulation affects a larger number of issues than at other times, and thus the general average of prices may be said to be partly dependent on manipulation.

But the fact should be remembered that both the public enthusiasm and the manipulation which accompanies it are the results of the conditions which made the bull market possible. Instances of manipulation purely at the will of some individual or group, regardless of current or prospective changes in actual conditions affecting values, are becoming more rare year by year, since it becomes more and more difficult to make such manipulations profitable.

In some commission offices, there are traders who, as a rule, go against whatever the outside customers of the house are doing. When members of the firm say, "all our customers are getting long of stocks," these traders sell out; but they buy when the firm says, "the customers are all short." There are, of course, exceptions to this rule. If there were no exceptions, the keepers of bucket shops would all get rich. When the market has an extraordinary rise, the public makes money, in spite of beginning its purchases at what would ordinarily be the wrong time, and this is when the bucket shops either lose their money or close out in order to keep such money of customers as they have in hand.

All this points to the soundness of the Rothschild principle of buying a property of known value when the public generally is disposed to sell; or of selling it when the public thinks it a time to buy.

Daniel Drew used to say, "cut your losses short, but let your profits run." This was good preaching, but "Uncle Dan" did not, in his later years, practice this rule, when it would have been better for him if he had. The thought here is unquestionably one of the sound principles in trading. It means that if a stock has been purchased and it goes up, it is well to wait; but if it goes down, it is well to stop the loss quickly on the ground that the theory on which the purchase was made was wrong.

The public, as a whole, exactly reverses this rule. The average operator, when he sees two or three points profit, takes it; but if a stock goes against him two or three points, he holds on waiting for the price to recover, with, oftentimes, the result of seeing a loss of two or three points run into a loss of ten points. He then becomes discouraged and sells out near the bottom to protect the margin which he has left.

How many operators in looking over their books find a considerable number of small profits swept away by one large loss? When a trader finds by his accounts that his profits have been relatively large and his losses relatively small, he can make up his mind that he is learning how to trade.

The trouble with carrying out this plan is that a series of losses of from $1\frac{1}{2}$ to 2 points are very discouraging. A trader who sees that he has taken twice or three times a loss of two points when, if he had waited a few days he need not have taken any loss, is very apt to decide that he will not cut his losses short any more, but will wait, and this is the time when the recovery does not come.

Mr. Jay Gould said his policy was to endeavor to foresee future conditions in a property and then, having made his commitments carefully, to exercise great patience in awaiting results. This also is sound doctrine, but proceeds along very different lines. Assuming the ability to foresee the future, it is the wisest of all courses; but many who have tried this method have found that the omission of essential factors made their forecast valueless, and both their courage and their patience of little avail. Nevertheless, this method should not be discarded on account of the difficulties involved. Within limitations, the future can be foreseen. The present is always tending toward the future and there are always in existing conditions signals of danger or encouragement for those who read with care.

CHAPTER II.

THE TWO GENERAL METHODS OF TRADING.

THERE are two general methods of trading. One is to deal in active stock in comparatively large amounts, relying for protection upon stop orders. In this method of trading it is not necessary to know much about the values. The point of chief importance is that the stock should be active enough to permit the execution of the stop order at the point selected so as to cut losses short.. The operator, by this method, guesses which way the stock will move. If he guesses right, he lets his profits run. If he guesses wrong, he goes out on the stop order. If he can guess right as often as he can guess wrong he is fairly sure of profits.

The other system is an entirely different proposition. It starts with the assumption that the operator knows approximately the value of the stock in which he proposes to deal. It assumes that he has considered the tendency of the general market; that he realizes whether the stock in which he proposes to deal is relatively up or down, and that he feels sure of its value for at least months to come.

Suppose this to exist: The operator lays out his plan of campaign on the theory that he will buy his first lot of stock at what he considers the right price and the right time, and will then buy an equal amount every 1 per cent. down as far as the decline may go.

This method of trading is the one generally employed by large operators. They know the value of the stock in which they propose to deal, and are therefore reasonably secure in following a decline. They feel about a stock as merchants feel about buying staple goods. If an article is cheap at $100, they know it is cheaper at $90, and will strain a point to buy at $80 or at $70, knowing that the price must recover. This is the way a large operator looks at his favorite stocks and this is why he generally makes money in them.

The disadvantage of the small operator in following this method is two-fold. He does not absolutely know the value of the stock. That is, he may know the truth up to a certain point, but beyond that is an unknown factor which interferes with the result. When the price of a stock declines considerably, the small operator always fears that he has overlooked something of importance, and he is therefore tempted to sell instead of averaging his holdings.

The second disadvantage of the small operator in following this policy is that he seldom provides sufficient capital for his requirements. Thousands of speculators believe that because 10 per cent. is a common speculative margin, $1,000 justifies them in trading in hundred share lots. This impression produces losses continually.

The man who has $1,000 for speculation is not well equipped for trading in even 10 share lots, if he proposes to deal on a scale. A comparison of high and low prices of active stocks shows frequently a difference of 30 points in a year. Any operator proposing to follow a stock down, buying on a scale, should make his preparations for a possible fall of from 20 to 30 points. Assuming that he does not begin to buy until his stock is 5 points down from the top, there is still a possibility of having to buy 20 lots before the turn will come.

If, however, an outsider will provide $2,500, as his speculative capital and will trade in ten-share lots in a thoroughly good railroad stock, beginning his purchases only after a decline of five points in a rising market, and ten points in a bear market, following the decline with purchases every point down, and retaining all the stock bought, he seldom need make a loss. (*See Note* 2.)

Such campaigns require time, patience, and the pursuance of a fixed policy, but whoever will follow this policy will find himself able to get a high rate of interest on the capital invested. It is an old saying in Wall Street that the man who begins to speculate in stocks with the intention of making a fortune, usually goes broke, whereas the man who trades with a view of getting good interest on his money, sometimes gets rich.

This is only another way of saying that money is made by conservative trading rather than by the effort to get large profits by taking large risks. After allowing for all the risks involved, we think the outsider who wants to trade in

NOTE 2.—There has been a great change in the character of the market since these paragraphs were written. What Mr. Dow said is still true of a large number of low and medium priced stocks which have sound investment value behind them. But many other issues, selling at a higher price or having a more speculative character, now have much wider fluctuations than those here mentioned and would require a correspondingly larger capital in proportion to the number of shares bought.

stocks has a better chance working in small lots on a scale than in any other way, provided he will pay attention to certain essential points, which for convenience of reference we will enumerate in order.

1.—Bull markets and bear markets run four and five years at a time. Determine by the average prices, which one is under way. (*See Note* 3.)

2.—Determine the stock or stocks to trade in. They should be railroad stocks, dividend payers, not too low, nor too high, fairly active, and for the bull side below their value; for the bear side above their value. Values are determined roughly by the earnings available for dividends. (*See Note.* 4.)

3. Observe the position of your stock with relation to recent fluctuations. In a bull market,

NOTE 3.—In recent years the average duration of bull and bear markets has been shorter than here indicated. See "Tidal Swings of the Stock Market," by Scribner Browne, published by *The Magazine of Wall Street.*

NOTE 4.—At the time this was written the industrial issues were comparatively new and were regarded as more speculative than the rails. Industrial stocks suited to this purpose could now be selected.

SCIENTIFIC STOCK SPECULATION.

the time to begin to buy is when a stock has had four or five points decline from the last previous top. In a bear market, the time to begin to sell is when such a stock has had three or four points rally from the bottom.

4.—Stick to the stock bought until a fair profit or until there is good reason for deciding that the first estimate of value was wrong. Remember that an active stock will generally rally from three-eighths to five-eighths of the amount of its decline under adverse conditions and more than that under favorable conditions.

5.—Have money enough to see a decline through without becoming uneasy or over-burdened; $2,500 ought to take care of a ten-share scale every point down—that is to say, supposing the first lot to be bought five points down from the top, $2,500 ought to carry the scale until the natural recovery from the low point brings the lot out with a profit on the average cost. It will not do to expect a profit on every lot, but only on the average. In a bull market it is better to always work on the bull side; in a bear market, on the bear side. There are usually more rallies in a bear market than there are relapses in a bull market. (*See Note* 5.)

Note 5.—As affecting more recent markets, this statement seems open to question.

6.—Do not let success in making money in ten-share lots create a belief that a bolder policy will be wiser and begin to trade in 100-share lots with inadequate capital. A few hundred-share losses will wipe out a good many ten-share profits.

7.—There is not usually much difficulty in dealing in ten-share lots on the short side. If one broker does not wish to do it, another probably will, especially for a customer who amply protects his account and who seems to understand what he is doing.

CHAPTER III.

THRFE GENERAL LINES OF REASONING.

WE have spoken in a preceding article of the fact that the experience of great interests in the market seems to have crystalized into three general lines of reasoning. The first is that the surface appearance of the market is apt to be deceptive. The second is that it is well in trading to cut losses short and let profits run. The third is that correctly discounting the future is a sure and easy road to wealth. The problem is how these rules which are undoubtedly sound, can be operated in a practical way.

Let us take first the action of the general market with reference to the time to buy. The market is always to be considered as having three movements, all going on at the same time. The first is the narrow movement from day to day. The second is the short swing, running from two weeks to a month or more; the third is the main movement covering at least four years in its duration. (*See Note* 3, *p.* 21.)

The day to day movement should be disregarded by everybody, except traders who pay no commissions. The medium swing is the one for ordinary consideration. The outside trader should not attempt to deal in more than two or three stocks at a time. He should keep a chart of the price movements of these stocks so as to know their swings for months or years, and thus be able to tell readily where in the general swing his particular stocks appear to be.

He should keep with his price movement a record of the volume of transactions and notes of any special facts bearing on that property, such as increases or decreases in earnings, increases in fixed charges, development of floating debt, and above all the actual earnings available for dividends as shown from month to month. He should observe the movement of the general market as indicated by the average published daily, as this shows the market more clearly than it is shown by any one stock. (*See Note 6.*)

The main purpose of this study is to enable the trader to determine, first, the value of the

Note 6.—Daily averages of the market are now published by various newspapers. Among the best are those of the New York *Times* and the *Wall Street Journal.*

stock he is in; whether it is increasing or decreasing and, second, when the time to buy seems opportune. Assuming the thirty day swing to be about five points, it is in the highest degree desirable not to buy when three of these points have passed, as such a purchase limits the probable profit to about two points.

It is therefore generally wise to look for a low point on a decline. Suppose, for instance, that Union Pacific was the stock under consideration; that it was clearly selling below its value, and that a bull market for the four-year period was under way. Assuming further that in a period of reaction Union Pacific had fallen four points from the previous highest. Assume earnings and prospects to be favorable and the outlook for the general market to be about normal. (*See Note 7.*)

This would be the time to begin to buy Union Pacific. The prudent trader, however, would take only part of his line. He would buy perhaps one-half of the stock he wanted and then give an order to buy the remainder as the price declined. The fall might go much further than he anticipated. It might be necessary to wait

NOTE 7.—Written, of course, before the excited fluctuations of Union Pacific, under the Harriman régime.

a long time for profit. There might even be developments which would make it wise to throw over the stock bought with the hope of replacing it materially lower.

These, however, are all exceptions. In a majority of cases this method of choosing the time to buy, founded upon clear perception of value in the stock chosen and close observation of the market swings under way will enable an operator to secure stock at a time and at a price which will give fair profits on the investment.

CHAPTER IV.

Swings Within Swings.

A CORRESPONDENT asks: "For some time you have been writing rather bullish on the immediate market, yet a little bearish in a larger sense. How do you make this consistent?"

We get this question in one form or another rather frequently. It denotes a lack of familiarity with fluctuations in prices when viewed over considerable periods. Many people seem to think that the change in prices in any one day is complete in itself and bears no relation to larger movements which may be under way. This is not so.

Nothing is more certain than that the market has three well defined movements which fit into each other. The first is the daily variation due to local causes and the balance of buying or selling at that particular time. The secondary movement covers a period ranging from ten days to sixty days, averaging probably between thirty and forty days. The third move is the great swing covering from four to six years.

In thinking about the market, it is necessary to think with reference to each of these periods in order to take advantage of opportunities. If the main move is up, relapses are speculators' opportunities, but if the main move is down, rallies furnish these opportunities.

Losses should not generally be taken on the long side in a bull period. Nor should they generally be taken on the short side in a bear period. It is a bull period as long as the average of one high point exceeds that of previous high points. It is a bear period when the low point becomes lower than the previous low points. It is often difficult to judge whether the end of an advance has come because the movement of prices is that which would occur if the main tendency had changed. Yet, it may only be an unusually pronounced secondary movement.

The first thing for any operator to consider is the value of the stock in which he proposes to trade. The second is to determine the direction of the main movement of prices. We know of nothing more instructive on this point than the course of prices as printed daily. The third thing is to determine the position of the secondary swing.

Assume for instance that the stock selected was Union Pacific; that the course of prices afforded clear evidence of a bull market under way; that the high point in Union Pacific thirty days ago was 108; that the price had slowly declined in sympathy with the market and without special new features to 98. The chances would be in favor of buying a part of the line wanted at that price with the intention of buying a little more if the stock had further decline or if the price showed a well defined advancing tendency. It would then be wise to watch the general market and wait for an advance.

A 10-point decline under such conditions would be almost certain to bring, in a bull market, more than five points recovery and full ten points would not be unreasonable; hence if the general market maintained a good tone, it would be wise to wait for five points and then begin to think about stop orders.

Even in a bear market, this method of trading will be usually be found safe, although the profit taken should be less because of the liability of weak spots breaking out and checking the general rise.

CHAPTER V.

METHODS OF READING THE MARKET.

A CORRESPONDENT writes: "Is there any way of forecasting the course of the market from the tape, from your records of transactions or from the summarized movement of prices? Transactions must mean something, but how can a trader tell what they mean?"

This is an old question. There have been a variety of answers but it is doubtful if any have been or can be wholly satisfactory. Several methods, however, are in practical use and at times afford suggestions.

There is what is called the book method. Prices are set down, giving each change of one point as it occurs, forming thereby lines having a general horizontal direction but running into diagonals as the market moves up and down. There come times when a stock with a good degree of activity will stay within a narrow range of prices, say two points, until there has formed quite a long horizontal line of these figures. The formation of such a line sometimes suggests that stock has been accumulated or distributed, and

33

this leads other people to buy or sell at the same time. Records of this kind kept for the last fifteen years seem to support the theory that the manipulation necessary to acquire stock is oftentimes detected in this way.

Another method is what is called the theory of double tops. Records of trading show that in many cases when a stock reaches top it will have a moderate decline and then go back again to near the highest figures. If after such a move, the price again recedes, it is liable to decline some distance.

Those, however, who attempt to trade on this theory alone find a good many exceptions and a good many times when signals are not given.

There are those who trade on the theory of averages. It is true that in a considerable period of time the market has about as many days of advance as it has of decline. If there comes a series of days of advance, there will almost surely come the balancing days of decline.

The trouble with this system is that the small swings are always part of the larger swings, and while the tendency of events equally liable to happen is always toward equality, it is also true that every combination possible is liable to occur, and there frequently come long swings, or, in the case of stock trading, an extraordinary

number of days of advance or decline which
fit properly into the theory when regarded on
a long scale, but which are calculated to upset
any operations based on the expectation of a series of short swings.

A much more practicable theory is that founded on the law of action and reaction. It seems
to be a fact that a primary movement in the
market will generally have a secondary movement in the opposite direction of at least three-
eighths of the primary movement. If a stock
advances ten points, it is very likely to have a
relapse of four points or more. The law seems
to hold good no matter how far the advance
goes. A rise of twenty points will not infrequently bring a decline of eight points or more.

It is impossible to tell in advance the length of
any primary movement, but the further it goes,
the greater the reaction when it comes, hence the
more certainty of being able to trade successfully
on that reaction.

A method employed by some operators of large
experience is that of responses. The theory involved is this: The market is always under more
or less manipulation. A large operator who is
seeking to advance the market does not buy
everything on the list, but puts up two or three
leading stocks either by legitimate buying or by

manipulation. (*See Note* 8.) He then watches the effect on the other stocks. If sentiment is bullish, and people are disposed to take hold, those who see this rise in two or three stocks immediately begin to buy other stocks and the market rises to a higher level. This is the public response, and is an indication that the leading stocks will be given another lift and that the general market will follow.

If, however, leading stocks are advanced and others do not follow, it is evidence that the public

NOTE 8.—When this was written it was possible for a large operator to advance quotations by bidding for larger lots than were offered; that is, he could bid for 5,000 shares, all or none. This is perhaps the species of manipulation here referred to. Under the present rules of the Stock Exchange this cannot be done, since the bidder must accept any part (in hundred share lots) of the amount bid for.

A certain amount of manipulation is still possible by purchasing heavily of a certain stock in a very short time, regardless of what price has to be paid. In that way only the "resting" orders will be encountered, since other traders do not have time to put in new selling orders until after the move is over, and the quickness of the rise may discourage them from putting in selling orders at all.

is not disposed to buy. As soon as this is clear the attempt to advance prices is generally discontinued. This method is employed more particularly by those who watch the tape. But it can be read at the close of the day in the record of transactions* by seeing what stocks were put up within specified hours and whether the general market followed or not.

The best way of reading the market is to read from the standpoint of values. The market is not like a balloon plunging hither and thither in the wind. As a whole, it represents a serious, well considered effort on the part of far-sighted and well-informed men to adjust prices to such values as exist or which are expected to exist in the not too remote future. The thought with great operators is not whether a price can be advanced, but whether the value of property which they propose to buy will lead investors and speculators six months hence to take stock at figures ten to twenty points above present prices.

In reading the market, therefore, the main point is to discover what a stock can be expected to be worth three months hence and then to see whether manipulators or investors are advancing

*Wall Street Journal, or official Stock Exchange lists.

the price of that stock toward those figures. It is often possible to read movements in the market very clearly in this way. To know values is to comprehend the meaning of movements in the market.

CHAPTER VI.

THE OPERATION OF STOP ORDERS.

A CORRESPONDENT inquires: "My brokers advise me to protect my transactions by stop orders. It seems to me that stop orders may be good for brokers by giving them commissions, but they make customers take unnecessary losses. Do you advise speculators to give stop orders?"

Proof on this point is afforded by taking a large number of fluctuations and seeing how the average works out. We believe that for the margin trader, and especially the trader who operates rather more largely than he ought on the margin that he has, stop orders are wise. There are, however, many qualifications which should be kept in mind.

If a man is trading as a semi-investor, using fifty per cent. margin, depending on values for his profit and operating in harmony with the main tendency of the market, we do not think a stop order desirable. To explain this a little more fully: Suppose the movement of averages shows that the market is in a rising period, such periods usually covering several years with only temporary reversals in direction. Suppose that an operator finds that a certain stock is earning an abnormal percentage on its market value, or, in other words, is intrinsically cheap. Suppose on the occasion of a temporary setback this stock is bought to be carried for months if necessary until the price has risen to approximately the level of the value. A stop order is folly in a case of this kind with anything like fair margin.

But, suppose a trader, having a margin of two or three thousand dollars, wants to trade in and out of stocks without regard to values, but being governed by points or by impressions of what the general market is going to do. Experience has shown that such a trader will, in the end, profit by putting a stop order about two points from the price at which he goes in. If there is advice that a stock is going up and it instead goes down two points without some obviously good reason for such a decline, the advice was not good, and the quicker the speculator lets go the better.

It often happens that when a stock moves two points it moves more, and it is a peculiarity of the human mind to disregard a small loss, but to get frightened and take a large loss just when wisdom would call for averaging a purchase.

Thousands of traders have said at two points

loss that they would see that particular transaction through if the stock went to nothing, only to decide after it had declined ten points that there was good reason for believing that it would decline ten more and acting accordingly. The experience of most traders is that the small losses occasioned by stop orders have a tendency to check their trading with a small aggregate loss, while the practice of letting a loss run not infrequently makes a loss so large that trading comes to an end because the speculator has no more money.

The maxim "let your profits run, but cut your losses short" has received the approval of most of the great stock operators. The authorship of the maxim has been credited to a dozen people, and most of them would have been willing to father it, although the great fortunes in stocks have not usually been made by people who give stop orders. Their opinion that stop orders were wise was based on their observation of people who tried to trade with insufficient capital, to whom stop orders especially apply.

The great profits in stocks have almost invariably been made by people who saw the tendency of events clearly and who then bought a large amount of stock which they thought certain to get the results of great increase in prosperity. Such stock has either been paid for out-right or very heavily margined, and then it has been held for months or years until great profits accrued.

Take the opportunities that have occurred in the last six years, or since 1896. Any one of from twenty to forty stocks could have been bought around 20 and sold above 80, and in at least half the cases above par, within that time. Such great opportunities do not come every year, but there are few times when some stocks can-not be pointed out as being lower in price than in value and as entitled to advance.

In a close speculative sense, a stop order is often useful. Stocks may be bought just when a reaction is setting in. In this case, it is fre-quently wise to take a quick loss on the theory that the reaction is likely to be five or six points, and that the stock can be recovered with a net saving of two or three points. A stop order is of no use to out-of town traders, because some-times the market moves a good deal before a broker can communicate with his client and get an order to act. Stop orders are often valuable on the short side of the market, because a scare of shorts after considerable decline sometimes brings a very rapid rise, which runs away with all the profits that have accrued.

Customers who give stop orders should, however, understand exactly what they mean. A customer who, being long of Union Pacific at 105, should give an order to stop at 103, would in effect be saying to the broker: "Whenever Union Pacific sells at 103, sell my stock immediately at the best price obtainable."

If the best price obtainable were 102 or even 101, the broker would still be within his rights in executing the order. Hence, in giving stop orders, thought should be taken as to the size of the market in the stock. In Union Pacific, for instance, a stop order ought to be executed within $\frac{1}{8}$ or $\frac{1}{4}$ per cent. of the stop order price, except in cases of panic, but a stop order in Lackawanna or Chicago & Eastern Illinois or in some industrial stock would be very dangerous, because no approximate idea could be formed as to what price would have to be accepted. (*See Note* 4, *p.* 21.)

Stop orders should not be given in any case in stocks of very limited market. In other stocks, their value will be found to depend largely upon the methods employed by the trader himself.

CHAPTER VII.

CUTTING LOSSES SHORT.

WE have spoken in previous articles of methods of trading. Experience proves that every operator should adopt one of two methods: Either cut losses short, or take an investment position. We propose to point out today some of the advantages of cutting losses short.

The buyer of any stock has some reason for his action. He has heard that the stock is going up; he believes that it is selling below its value, he sees that a bull market is under way and believes that this stock will go up as much as any other. These and similar reasons lead to buying.

It is obvious that in all but one of these cases the buyer does not profess to know anything definitely about the stock he buys. He acts on the suggestions or advice of others. Points are good when they are good, and under some conditions can very wisely be followed. There is nothing better in trading than to know that a great operator or a great syndicate intends for good reasons to move the price of a stock from a lower to a higher figure.

But almost everybody learns by sad experience that the "best laid plans of mice and men gang aft agley." Great operators change their minds about the expediency of market movements and most of them have learned that it is one thing to will and another to do in stock speculation. Hence the trader who takes a point, even from good sources, has only partial assurance of profitable results.

His true protection in such a case lies in a stop order. If the price advances, well and good, but if it declines his stop order cuts his loss short, while those who do not stop the loss, but who listen to assurances that the market is all right, often see larger losses in the end.

The general rule is to stop losses within a range of two or three points from the purchase price. All purchases on points, tendencies and rumors should be regarded as guesses and protected by stop orders. Traders, looking over their accounts, seldom lament the losses of $200, which they find scattered through their books as the result of stops, but they deeply lament the $1,500 or the $2,500 losses which reflect over-confidence in a position which proved unsound.

The difficulty with stop orders is that they are frequently exercised when the event shows that the loss need not have been taken. There is no help for this, but the placing of a stop order can be wisely varied by the circumstances of a given case. Suppose, for instance, that the five-year movement showed a bull market to be in progress; that there has come in this advance a five-point reaction in a stock like Union Pacific and that a purchase had been made five points from the previous highest.

If the price declined two points more in such a case, it would probably be wise to exercise the stop order as the fall would suggest a down swing of larger proportions than had been anticipated. It might be such a move as occured in December, 1899, when stop orders proved exceedingly profitable in bull accounts. If the price subsequently recovered the two points, and the stock was repurchased at about the original price, it would probably be wise to put the stop order the next time about three points away, under a belief that the stock would not go quite so low as it went before and that the stop order would therefore not be executed.

If this reasoning proved sound, and the price advanced the stop order could wisely be kept three points below the market price until the stock had advanced several points and showed signs of what is called "toppiness." Then it might be well to advance the stop order to two points and await developments.

The stop order is of primary importance when a purchase is first made and when its wisdom is in doubt. It is also of primary importance in pyramiding; that is, where stock is being bought on an advancing market every point up, because in such a case the stop order is relied upon to prevent the turning of a profit into a loss. It is of importance when a stock has had its normal swing for the purpose of saving most of the profit if a reaction comes, while leaving a chance open for further advance. It is of least importance when a stock has been well bought and is slowly advancing. It should be set further away from the market at such a time than any other so as to avoid being caught on the small setbacks which occur in an advancing period.

By means of a stop order, an operator can trade freely in active stocks of uncertain value, which he would not venture to touch as an investment. By it, he can trade in much larger amounts than he could otherwise undertake to protect. The stop order is the friend of the active speculator, who wants to make a quick dash for a large profit and who is willing to make small losses in the hope of getting a good run once in four or five attempts. It is the friend of the small operator, the out-of-town, operator and the timid operator. It should be applied, however, only in active stocks where there is a large market. Stop orders should not be given in inactive stocks, as the seller may be slaughtered in their execution.

A stop order to sell 100 shares of Union Pacific at 75 means that the stock must be sold at the best price obtainable as soon as there has been a transaction at 75. If the best price were 74 or 73, it would still be the duty of the broker to sell. Hence the importance of not giving such orders in stocks where wide differences in quotations may be expected.

CHAPTER VIII.

The Danger in Overtrading.

A FREQUENT inquiry is: "Can I trade in stocks on a capital of $100, buying on a scale up and stopping my loss so as to protect my original capital?"

There are a great many people in the United States who think about trading in stocks on a capital of $100 or $200. Many of them believe that if a thousand dollars is a proper 10 per cent. margin for trading in 100 shares, $100 must be a fair margin for trading in 10 shares. We regard this reasoning as sound, but dissent from the conclusion that $1,000 justifies trading in 100 share lots.

The reason is that nobody can hope to buy at the bottom or to sell at the top; or to be right all the time or to avoid losses. Making money in stocks for most people resolves itself into a series of transactions in which we may say there are six profits and four losses, resulting in a net gain. The experience of good traders shows that the operating expenses in trading, that is to say,

the ratio of losses to profits, run from 50 to 65
per cent. of the total profits.

A man who may have made $10,000 gross
in trading in a specified time will be very likely
to have lost from $5,000 to $6,000 gross in the
same time, leaving a net profit of from $4,000 to
$5,000. Profits and losses run in streaks. There
will be times of all profit and no loss, and times
of all loss and no profit. But the average even
for those who have learned to trade in stocks and
who have abundant capital for their operations
works out less than half of the gross profits as
net profits.

What chance is there for 10 per cent. to carry
a speculator and especially a beginner through
the losses which are almost certain to come before he can accumulate any substantial profit?
It is possible to say that if an operator had done
this or that, buying at the right time and selling
at the right time, 10 per cent. would have been
ample. But, there is a great difference between
seeing what might have been done in the past
and undertaking to do something for the future.

The man who wishes to trade in stocks and
who has only $100 to lose, should, in our opinion,
adopt one of two courses. He should buy out-
right one share of some stock below par and
below its value and wait until the advance in that

stock to its value gives him a profit of 5 to 10 per cent. as the case may be. This is probably the surest way.

The other way is to buy two or three shares on margin, protecting the account by a stop order at about two points from the purchase price. Brokers generally are not anxious to take such small lots, but if a broker believes that a customer is trading on right lines, and is likely to make money, he will go out of his way considerably to serve that customer, under a belief that he will be worth something in the future. Nine brokers out of ten would say that an attempt to trade in stocks on a capital of $100 was absurd. But, it would not be absurd if the trading basis were made two shares, as that would give the trader time in which to recover from his losses as well as some confidence in acting at the proper time and would be a sort of school in which experience could be gained.

We think exactly the same reasoning holds good with regard to trading in 100-share lots on a basis of $1,000. Some brokers accept such orders readily enough, but it is none the less over-trading, and none the less likely to result in the loss of the trader's capital. The man who buys 100 shares on a 10 per cent. margin and stops his loss at two points, has lost nearly one-quarter of his capital. He tries again and perhaps makes one point net. His third venture results in a loss of three points more and in a nearly total loss of confidence, leading him probably to sell short just when he ought to have averaged, thereby completing the sacrifice of his money.

If the same man with a capital of $1,000 had begun with 10 shares he could have stood his loss; he would have had courage to average or to buy something else at a low point and would very likely come out ahead.

Almost any man can show profits in a stock by assuming that he would do so and so at various conditions of the market. He succeeds theoretically in this way because there is nothing at risk and his judgment is clear. The moment, however, that he has a risk which is very large in proportion to his capital, he consults his fears instead of his judgment, and does in practice exactly opposite what he would have done had his transactions been purely academic.

The remedy for this is to keep transactions down to a point, as compared with capital, which leaves the judgment clear and affords ample ability to cut loss after loss short; to double up; to take hold of something else, and generally to act easily and fearlessly instead of under the

constraint which inevitably comes from a knowledge that the margin of safety is so small as to
leave no room for anything except a few anxious
gasps before the account is closed.

If people with either large or small capital
would look upon trading in stocks as an attempt
to get 12 per cent. per annum on their money
instead of 50 per cent. weekly, they would come
out a good deal better in the long run. Everybody knows this in its application to his private
business, but the man who is prudent and careful
in carrying on a store, a factory or a real estate
business seems to think that totally different
methods should be employed in dealing in stocks.
Nothing is further from the truth.

CHAPTER IX.

METHODS OF TRADING.

A CORRESPONDENT inquires: "How can a man living at a distance from Wall Street hope to follow the market closely enough to make any money trading in stocks?"

This question comes to us in different forms frequently, and shows misapprehensions as to what is involved in successful trading. Many people seem to think that if an operator is in Wall Street, he can tell what the market is going to do. Nothing is further from the fact. The more a man really knows about speculation, the less certain he becomes in regard to any market movement, except as the result of general conditions.

The distinction to be made between trading in the Street and trading from out of town is clear in one point. The operator who watches the ticker or blackboard can turn at very short notice, but the ability to turn quickly often proves a great disadvantage, because it leads to many turns at the wrong time.

The out-of-town speculator should not attempt

to make quick turns, unless by private wire connections he is able to watch the market as a matter of business. The out-of-town operator should trade on broad lines and from an investment standpoint. He should deal not in stocks that happen to be active, and not on points but almost wholly on well considered convictions as to the probable course of the general market and the relative position of price to value of the special stocks in which he proposes to deal.

The first question to consider is what constitutes a speculative investment. We should say it meant in most cases a railway stock paying regular dividends, publishing earnings, gross and net, at regular intervals and giving full particulars of its financial and physical condition as often at least as once a year. If oftener, so much the better. (*See Note* 4, *p.* 21.)

It is possible to derive fairly accurate knowledge of the value of such a stock. It should be considered essentially with reference to its ability to maintain or increase its dividends. If the stock seems likely to continue a current rate of dividend, and the return on the cost is such as to make it fairly satisfactory as an investment, it is a good stock to buy when, in sympathy with decline in the general market, it has fallen below its normal price.

Take, for instance, Union Pacific common. A few months ago this stock was selling between 50 and 60. It was paying 4 per cent. dividends, and the company was known to be earning over 8 per cent. Here was the case of a stock obviously selling below its value. It has since risen more than 30 points. There were other stocks, perhaps not as cheap in point of value, but of which much that was favorable could be said. Three months ago the values of railway stocks generally were above their prices.

Now, this can be said of very few stocks, and this fact ought to make an outsider slow to buy. The chances are that there will come, as there seems to be coming, declines which will carry prices back to a level where it will again be prudent to buy. Suppose that time to arrive. The wise course for an outsider will be to buy of a good railroad stock, an amount he can easily purchase outright, and which he would be willing to hold as an investment in case the price should decline. Should it then decline considerably it would probably be prudent for him to buy more lowering his average, but only after careful revision of the facts bearing upon the value and upon the general market.

This stock should be held without regard to current fluctuations, until it showed a satisfactory profit. Then it should be sold and the operator should wait weeks or months if necessary for an opportunity to take it or some other stock back upon favorable terms.

The outsider who tries to follow the market from day to day, is not likely to have very marked success. The operator who selects investment properties carefully and buys after the market has had general declines, and who exercises a good deal of patience both in waiting for the time to buy and for the time to sell—who, in short, treats his speculation as an investment, will be likely to make money in stocks as a rule.

A correspondent writes: "Is there any way by which an outsider who cannot watch fluctuations of the market hourly can trade in stocks with a fair chance of making money?"

We think there are two methods by either of which an outsider has a fair speculative chance. The first is to buy stocks for investment; that is, to pay for them outright when they are selling below value and wait until they are up to value, getting the difference for a profit.

Value is determined by the margin of safety over dividends, the size and tendency of earnings; the soundness of the balance sheet and of operating methods, and general prospects for the future. This sounds rather complicated, but is not especially difficult to work out.

For instance, a year ago we almost daily pointed out that earnings had greatly increased during the year past; that fixed charges had not increased, hence that the actual value of stocks had advanced while prices had in most cases declined.. It was obvious that this could not last; that net earnings must decrease or prices advance. There were then many stocks cheap on their earnings and this was easily a matter of demonstration.

In the same sense it can now (1902) be said that most stocks are dear on their earnings. It is true that earnings have increased somewhat over last year, but prices of many stocks have advanced from 50 to 100 per cent., and in whatever form the yardstick is applied the result is unfavorable to value as compared with prices in a large number of the active stocks.

When a stock sells at a price which returns only about $3\frac{1}{2}$ per cent. on the investment, it is obviously dear, except there be some special reason for the established price. In the long run, the prices of stocks adjust themselves to the return on the investment and while this is not a safe guide at all times it is a guide that should never be laid aside or overlooked. The tendency of prices over a considerable length of time will always be toward values. Therefore, the outsider who by studying earning conditions can approach a fairly correct idea of value has a guide for his investments which will, as a whole, be found safe.

Most people, however, when they talk about making money in stocks do not mean the slow road through investments but the short cut by way of speculation. We think here again there is one rule worth all others on this subject. It is a rule which is carried out with greater or less precision by a majority of successful traders. It has been approved by the practical experience of almost everybody who has dealt at all freely in stocks.

This rule is to cut losses short but let profits run. It sounds very easy to follow, but is in reality difficult to observe. The difficulty arises from the unwillingness of an operator to take a small loss when experience shows him that in many cases such a loss need not have been taken. Furthermore, the practice of this rule suggests that having, for instance, bought a stock and taken a loss, the stock should be bought again, and this may have to be done three or four times before an advance finally comes. These three or four losses prove very burdensome and lead people oftentimes to decide not to cut the loss short and that is generally when a large loss ensues.

The question will of course be asked whether there should be a uniform stop loss, or whether it should vary with varying conditions. Experience indicates that two points is the wisest place to stop a loss. If a stock goes two points against the buyer, it is very liable to go more, and it suggests that the expected move has either been delayed or is not coming.

Suppose, for instance, that an operator believes from information, study of values, experience in markets and the tendency of the period, that Union Pacific ought to be bought at 107. If he buys at that price and the stock falls to 105, theoretically he should cut his loss, buying it again when the indications are again favorable.

Extended records of trading show that this policy, blindly followed, with blind following also of the plan of letting profits run, would give better results than most people are able to obtain by the exercise of judgment. At the same time, judgment can sometimes be wisely employed in cutting a loss.

It is not, for instance, necessary in all cases to take a loss because the price is suddenly jammed down two points. If the market shows a tendency to rally, wait a little. If a decline in the stock bought is obviously due to a collapse in some other stock, and that collapse seems to have spent its force, it would be necessary to execute the stop. The idea is to stop the loss when the market has legitimately declined to that extent.

In letting profits run there are two ways of determining when to close. One is to wait until the general market shows a decided change of temper. The other is to keep a stop order about three points behind the high prices on the advance and close on that stop. Here, again, experience has shown that when a stock starts on a manipulated advance, it is seldom allowed to react as much as three points until the move is completed. If it reacts three points, it may mean trouble with the deal, although there are cases where such reactions are allowed for the purpose of shaking out following. Here, again, something can be left to judgment.

But the great thing is having bought a stock and having got fairly away from the purchase price, not to be in too great a hurry about selling, provided that the general market is bullish. In a bear market, the whole proceeding ought to be reversed, the operator taking the short side instead of the long, but in other respects applying the same rule.

We do not wish to be understood as saying that there is any sure way of making money in stocks, but the principle of buying after a period of steadiness in prices, stopping losses and letting profits run will, as a matter of statistical record, beat most people's guessing at what is going to occur. (*See Note* 9.)

NOTE 9.—While the principles stated in the latter part of this chapter are as good today as they were in 1902 the great broadening out of the market since then, the changed status of industrial issues and the number of high-priced stocks which are actively traded in, make the actual application of the principles subject to considerable modification.

In General Motors, for example, an issue which has unquestionable value behind it and which, at this writing, has an active market around 240, a two-point stop order would be absurd. In fact, there is often a gap of about two points between the bid and offered prices. Nevertheless, over 10,000 shares a day are being traded in. A stop order can be executed in this issue without much difficulty, but it would have to be placed farther away from the purchase price.

Baldwin Locomotive, again, is selling around 110 and has a close market, so that stops can be readily executed. But its usual fluctuations are too wide to make a two-point stop practicable, unless in a very quiet market.

Both stop orders and the averaging principle must be modified according to the nature of the stock traded in.

CHAPTER X.

The Out of Town Trader.

A CORRESPONDENT asks: "How can a man living at an interior city, where he sees quotations only once or twice a day, make money by trading in stocks?"

This question touches a point which seems to find wide-spread acceptance, namely, that proximity to Wall Street is a special advantage in trading. It certainly is for some kinds of trading. If a man owns a seat on the Stock Exchange and pays no commissions, he can probably do best by operating for his own account on the floor of the exchange, although not every man with these facilities is able to make his profits exceed his losses.

For practical purposes, it may be said that most traders in or out of Wall Street are handicapped by the commission of $25 for buying and selling 100 shares of stock. There probably are some evasions of the commission rule, but as ·far as individual operators are concerned, commissions are not much evaded.

A commission of $12.50 for buying and as much more for selling 100 shares of stock is insignificant if there are ten or even five points difference between the buying and selling price. But the commission is serious if the difference between the buying and the selling price is only one point. A man who started in to trade for one point profit and pays ⅛ commission would inevitably give all his money to his broker in the course of time. (*See Note* 10.)

The ordinary operator must always endeavor to get comparatively large profits. He should not

NOTE 10.—Present commission rates are $7.50 per 100 shares for stocks selling under $10, $15 per 100 for those selling from $10 to $125, and $20 per 100 for those selling at $125 or more. There is also a $2 U. S. Government tax and a $2 New York State tax on each sale of 100 shares, but no tax on purchases.

The trader also has the handicap of the "invisible eighth" or quarter between the bid and asked prices. If the market is 88 bid, 88⅛ asked, the buyer at the market will pay 88⅛ while the seller at the market will get only 88. On such an issue the trader who buys and sells at the market really starts with a loss of $46.50 on 100 shares of a stock selling from $10 to $125; that is, this is the loss he would suffer if he bought and sold at exactly the same moment.

buy unless he feels warranted in believing that the stock which he selects will go up four or five points, so that when he makes he will get double his loss when he loses. In trading for five or ten point turns, the operator at an interior city has one advantage. He does not hear the rumors and see sudden movements in prices which are the bane of the office trader.

Wall Street is often full of people to-day who have been long of the market for a month, but who have made little or no money, because they have been scared out by rumors and by small relapses. The man who does not see the market escapes this.

The greatest disadvantage resting upon the out of town operator is the fact that sometimes the market will change its character so rapidly as to convert a profit into a loss or establish a loss larger than he intended to take before he knows it. This, however, does not occur as frequently as most people seem to suppose.

It is rather exceptional for the market, having run several points in one direction, to reverse the movement suddenly and without considerable fluctuations near the turning points. Such cases do occur, but they are unusual. (*See Note* 11.)

Note 11.—These sudden turns are more common now than they were in 1902.

After a five-point rise, a stock usually has a period during which fluctuations are narrow and which are maintained long enough to give the out-of-town trader plenty of time to get out if he dislikes the appearance of the trading. Stop orders are the special protection of the out-of-town trader, who, if he will stick to stable stocks, can almost always cut his loss or save his profit at any spot where he deems wise.

The out-of-town trader wants to begin his campaign with a conviction that the stock which he buys is selling below its value. This should not only be a conviction, but a demonstrated conviction, which cannot be shaken if, at the outset, the price declines instead of advances. Having determined on his stock from the viewpoint of value, he should, if possible, wait about buying until the general market has had its normal setback from a high point.

If twenty active stocks have advanced 10 points, a normal setback would be four points, and then, in an extended period of rising prices, would be the time to make the initial purchase. The operator should then take in a great stock of patience. He will see other stocks go up and his stock stand still. He will see and hear daily that something else is making riches for traders, but he must shut his ears to these statements, even if they are right as far as fluctuations go. He must just sit on his stock, which is intrinsically below its value, until other people observe that it is selling too low and begin to buy it.

The tendency with most people holding a stock which does not move for a time is to sell the stock about as soon as it begins to move, through fear that it will again become dull. This is just the time not to sell, but, if anything, to buy more on the idea that other people have discovered that the price is below value. After the price has moved up two or three points, it is well to put in a stop order perhaps two points back from the top and follow the rise in the stock with the stop order, disregarding current reports and waiting until the price is either up to the value or until market conditions make taking a profit judicious, provided always that a sudden setback does not close out the transaction.

, An out-of-town operator can do all this just as well as an office trader and in some respects better. Some of the large operators like to go away from the market and work from Newport or Saratoga or other distant points in order to look at the trading with an unbiased mind and without being unsettled by the rumors that always grow out of any special move. The outsider who will wisely study values and market conditions and then exercise patience enough for six men will be likely to make money in stocks.

CHAPTER XI.

THE SHORT SIDE OF THE MARKET.

A CORRESPONDENT writes: "You demonstrate that an operator in stocks ought to work on the short side of the market during about half of almost every decade. I feel some hesitation about selling property which I do not own. Will you not make it clear how the short side of the market is normal trading?"

It is quite true that in each of the past four decades it would have been wise to work on the short side at least half of the time. It is also true that the public as a whole does not like short selling. It is true that corners occur at long intervals and are destructive to those caught therein. But they occur so seldom as to make them a very remote danger. There is about one in ten years. (*See Note* 12.)

NOTE 12.—Partial corners are far more common. By this is meant a condition of the market when the supply of stocks available in some issue becomes so small that only small amounts can be purchased without putting the price up far beyond the actual value.

We have explained the principle of short sell-
ing many times, but will state the process once
more.   Customer X directs Broker A to 'sell
short 100 shares of Union Pacific at par. Broker
B buys it.   A, not having the stock goes to
Broker C, and borrows from him 100 shares of
Union Pacific, giving as security $10,000 in cash.
This stock is then delivered by A to B, who pays
A $10,000 therefor. Matters then rest until Union
Pacific advances or declines enough to make X
wish to close his account.   He then directs A
to buy Union Pacific, say at 95, and A gets the
stock from Broker D.   The stock thus obtained
is delivered to C, who thereupon returns the
money which he has had as security and $9,500
of the amount goes to D, leaving $500, less ex-
penses, as the profit of X on the transaction.

While X is waiting to see what the market is
going to do C has the use of A's $10,000, and
under ordinary conditions, pays interest on this
money.   This interest is called the loaning rate
on stocks and is usually a little below the current
rate for loans on collateral.

The lower these rates are, compared with the
rate for money, the more demand there is to borrow that particular stock, and the loaning rate is
the point to be watched by those who may be
short, to see whether the short interest is large
or small.

In case the demand to borrow a certain stock is very large, the loaning rate will be quoted flat, which means in the case cited that C would get the use of A's $10,000 without paying any interest. If the demand for the stock should be still greater, A might have not only to give C the $10,000 without interest, but a small premium in addition. When the loaning rate of stock is quoted at 1-32 it means that C gets his $10,000 from A, without interest, and in addition a premium of $3.12 a day for each 100 shares, which has to be paid by X, who must also pay all dividends that may be declared on the stock.

In ordinary lines of business, selling short with the idea of borrowing for delivery would be impossible. In the stock market it is impracticable to sell distributed bonds or investment stocks short because such securities are held by investors, and are not carried in quantity by brokers, hence, could not be readily borrowed. But, in active stocks, there is no difficulty whatever in borrowing.

The reason is this: Every broker who carries many stocks employs a great deal more money than he possesses. In theory, a broker carrying for a customer 100 shares of Union Pacific at par would make up the money for the purchase by using $1,000 belonging to the customer, $1,000 of the money of the brokerage firm, and then borrow $8,000 from a bank on the security of the 100 shares of stock purchased.

An active broker, consequently, is always a large borrower of money, and when he borrows from a bank he is expected to put up 20 per cent. margin on his loan. But if he can lend stocks he gets the full value of the stock and does not have to put up any of his own money or of his customer's money. Hence, every broker is willing to lend stocks, particularly when the demand for stock is sufficient to make the rate of interest lower than the market rate, as the broker in this case makes a profit by charging his customer who is long five or six per cent. interest, while he perhaps secures his money without any cost through lending the stock flat.

This, from the standpoint of the short seller, is what makes his operation practically safe. Ordinarily, it is just as easy to borrow active stocks as it is to borrow money, and squeezes of shorts through inability to borrow stocks are little if any more frequent than squeezes of "longs" through the difficulty of brokers in borrowing money.

Squeezes of shorts sometimes develop themselves and are sometimes manipulated. When friends of a property see a large short interest they sometimes try to persuade holders of the stock to agree not to lend it for a day or two and thus scare shorts to cover by difficulty in borrowing. If this undertaking is successful brokers are notified to return borrowed stock, and when they try to borrow elsewhere they find little offering. The loaning rate possibly runs up to one-fourth per cent. a day, or perhaps higher.

Shorts are alarmed and cover, advancing the price of the stock and enabling holders to sell at a profit. Such a squeeze usually lasts only two or three days, as by that time the advanced price leads those who have the stock to either sell it or lend it, and the price then usually goes lower than before. Sometimes there is a short interest so large and so persistent as to keep a stock lending at a premium for some time. This is usually almost certain evidence of decline, but the expenses of premiums and the necessity of paying dividends sometimes eat up the profits so that but little remain even after considerable fall in price. Mr. Gould is said to have once remained short of New York Central over four years, and to have had a large profit as between his buying and his selling price, but to have had the greater part of it eaten up in dividends.

In picking out a stock to sell short, the first consideration ought to be that the price is above value, and that future value appears to be shrinking. It should be an active stock and, if possible, a stock of large capital. It should be an old stock by preference, which means having wide distribution instead of concentrated ownership. By preference it should be a high priced stock with a reasonable probability that dividends will be reduced or passed.

Such a stock should be sold on advances and bought in on moderate declines, say four or five points, as long as the market seems to be reasonably steady. But, if the market becomes distinctly weak, only part of the short stock should be bought in with the hope that some short interest may be established at a price so high as to be out of reach of temporary swings.

The best profits in the stock market are made by people who get long or short at extremes and stay for months or years before they take their profit.

CHAPTER XII.

SPECULATION FOR THE DECLINE.

THE question is frequently asked whether in taking a bearish view of the general market it is expected that all stocks will go down together or that some will fall and others not.

The answer to this question takes two forms—the first is the speculative movement; the second the effect of values. When the market goes down, especially if the decline is violent or continued, all stocks fall; not perhaps equally, but enough to be regarded as participating fully in a general decline. Indeed, it often happens that a stock of admitted large value will fall more in a panic than a stock of little value.

The reason is that when people have been carrying various stocks, some good and some bad, and a time comes when they are obliged to suddenly furnish additional margin or reduce their commitments, they try to sell the stocks for which they think the market will be best, namely, their best stocks. But the very merit of such stocks prevents the existence of a short interest, hence when considerable amounts are offered in a panic

there is no demand for covering purposes, and, in
fact, no demand x   from investors who may
have "resting" or "good until countermanded"
orders in the hands of their brokers, or who may
have money available for investment at that particular moment.

Consequently the stock drops until it meets
an investment demand somewhere. This condition was illustrated by the action of Delaware &
Hudson in the panic of May 9, 1901. It had
nearly, if not quite, the largest decline of any
stock on the list, falling in half an hour from 160
to 105, chiefly because people generally did not
know the price at which stock was being offered.

It may be accepted, therefore, that in a general
decline merit in a stock will not count for the
time being. Good and bad will decline measur-
ably alike. But here comes in a marked distinction. When the recovery comes, a day or a week
later, the good stock will recover more and hold
its recovery better than the poor stock. Delaware & Hudson is again a good illustration.
After the quotation of 105 was printed on May 9
orders to buy the stock came from all sections,
and in another hour the price was in the neighborhood of 150.

Value will always work out in the course of
time. A stock intrinsically cheap and a stock

intrinsically dear may be selling at the same price at a given time. As the result of six months' trading they may have presented the appearance of moving together in most of the fluctuations, but at the end of the period the good stock will be 10 points higher than the poor one, the difference representing a little smaller decline and a little better rally in each of five or six swings.

This exactly describes what will occur all through the market during the next bear period, whenever that period comes. There will be a sifting of the better from the worse, visible enough at a distance, but not conspicuous at any particular stage in the process.

. When there is a great change in the value of a stock it will advance in a bear period. The market as a whole declined from 1881 to 1885, but in that period Manhattan, while participating in most of the market swings, went from the neighborhood of 30 to the neighborhood of par, because the increased earnings of the company increased value steadily and largely during that time.

The practical lesson is that a stock operator should not deal in stocks unless he thinks he knows their value, nor unless he can watch conditions so as to recognize changes in value as they come along. He should then have at least a conviction as to what stocks are above their value and what are below their value at a given time. If the main tendency of the market is downward, he should sell stocks which he believes to be above their value when they are very strong, taking them in on the next general decline. In buying for a rally, he should invariably take the stocks that are below their value, selling them also when a moderate profit is shown.

When the market appears in a doubtful position it is sometimes wise to sell short a stock that is conspicuously above its value and buy a stock which is conspicuously below its value, believing that one will protect the other until the position of the general market becomes clear. It was formerly very popular for traders to be long of Northwest and short of St. Paul, usually with good results.

During the past year (1901-2) there have been operators who have aimed to be long of Manhattan and short of either Metropolitan or Brooklyn on the same line of reasoning. The general method of operating such an account is to trade for the difference; that is, supposing a transaction to have been started with the two stocks 10 points apart—the account is closed when they are, say, 15 points apart, assuring 5 points net profit. It is all, however, a part of the same general law. Stock fluctuate together, but prices are controlled by values in the long run.

CHAPTER XIII.

CONCERNING DISCRETIONARY ACCOUNTS.

A CORRESPONDENT writes: "I inclose herewith a circular in which the sender asks me to give him a discretionary account promising large returns and claiming great success in past operations. A man in the market ought to be able to do better for me than I could do for myself at a distance. Is this party reliable, and do you consider his scheme safe?"

We get this letter in some form very often and have answered it many times, but it is difficult to make people see the truth. Outsiders want to make money and they believe that people in Wall Street know what the market is going to do, hence that the only question involved in discretionary accounts is the honesty of the men who run them.

The fact is that people in Wall Street, even those who get very near the center of large operations, do not know what the market is going to do with any regularity or certainty. The more they actually know, the less confident they become, and the large operators who try to make markets are, in most cases, the least confident of anybody because they know so well the variety and extent of the difficulties which may be encountered.

People who trade in stocks can set down as a fundamental proposition the fact that any man who claims to know what the market is going to do any more than to say that he thinks this or that will occur as a result of certain specified conditions is unworthy of trust as a broker. Any man who claims that he can take discretionary accounts and habitually make money for his customers, is a fraud; first, because he knows when he makes such statements that he cannot do it regularly or with certainty, and, second, because if he could, he would surely trade for himself and would scorn working for one-eighth commission when he could just as well have the whole amount made.

The governors of the Stock Exchange will not permit a member of that body to advertise that he will take discretionary accounts, and any Stock Exchange member who stated that he was endeavoring to build up a business by discretionary trading for customers would lose caste with his fellow-members. It would be considered that he was either lacking in honesty or in judgment.

We do not say that Stock Exchange houses never take a discretionary account. They sometimes do, but they take them unwillingly in very limited amounts, only for people with whom they have very confidential relations and who understand speculation suffciently to expect losses and failures quite as frequently as profits. It is safe to say that Stock Exchange houses regard the acceptance of a discretionary account as a rather serious demand upon personal friendship, and this not because they do not wish to see their friends make money, but because they know too well that a discretionary account often means the loss of both money and friends.

When, therefore, men of little or no capital and little or no reputation advertise boldly in the Sunday papers that they desire discretionary accounts from strangers and will, for a commission of one-eighth per cent., guarantee profits ranging from 25 to 250 per cent. per annum, commission houses have but one word with which to describe the proposition and people of practical experience in Wall Street are amazed at the credulity of those who send their money to be placed in such accounts and who subsequently appear in the company of those who wail in the outer rooms of closed offices over the rascality which has robbed them of their hard earnings.

The head of a discretionary concern which was very prominent a year or two ago frequently said that if the United States Government would let his mails alone and deliver to him the money forwarded by his dupes he would ask no better occupation and no quicker road to wealth. Evidence presented in court has shown repeatedly that swindlers who have advertised to make money for the public in speculation have received thousands of letters containing money; that none of this money was ever invested in stocks; that the advertisers were not members of any exchange and did not even pretend to have any business other than receiving and keeping the bulk of the money entrusted to their care. A small amount of the money received was usually returned to senders as profits on alleged transactions.

This is substantially, we believe, the general practice. If a man sends $100 to one of the concerns, he is notified, after a little time, that he has made $10 and, a little later, that his share of a pool profit is $15. At this point he is usually advised to send $100 more on account of some extraordinary opportunity which has just arisen. If this money is sent, he is told that profits have accrued and still more money is called for. Persons who call for some of their profits are occasionally given money in order that the receiver may induce others to join the list of future victims.

The end, however, is almost, if not quite invariably, a communication stating that by some adverse and utterly unexpected fatality operations have been unsuccessful and the money invested has been lost. It is usually thought wise to make the victims appear somewhat in debt in order to induce them by not having to pay the alleged debt to accept as a mysterious dispensation of Providence the loss of their capital and previous alleged profits.

Speculation is not at its best a simple and easy road to wealth, but speculation through people who advertise guaranteed profits and who call for participation in blind pools is as certain a method of loss as could possibly be discovered. The mere fact that a man openly asks for such accounts is the most ample and exhaustive reason possible for declining to give them.

CHAPTER XIV.

THE LIABILITY FOR LOSS.

OF a number of inquiries lately the following is a sample: "I was long of stocks May 9, 1901, and was sold out. The broker now asks me to pay a loss in excess of my margin. Am I liable therefor?"

This question has never been definitely settled as a matter of law. There have been a good many decisions in cases of this kind but they have generally been sufficiently dissimilar to make each decision rest upon that particular case, and not as establishing a principle of law, bearing thereon.

Cases of this kind generally fall under one of two general divisions. Either the broker notifies his customer that his margin is nearly exhausted, or he does not. It is probably good law to assume that where a stock is bought on margin and, on a fall in the price, the broker calls on the customer for more margin and there is no response within a reasonable time, the broker is justified in selling the stock without a positive order to do so from the customer. The courts have held in such cases that the broker gave ample notice and the customer should have responded in time to protect his interests. The broker could not be expected to wait more than a reasonable time.

In cases of this class it sometimes happens that the customer does not think it wise to put up more margin and orders the stock sold. It may be sold at a loss on account of a rapid decline in prices. In this case, there seems to be little doubt of the liability of the customer, because the broker is executing an order to sell for the account and risk of that customer. Here, however, might enter special questions as to whether the broker was or was not negligent in notifying the customer that margin was needed, or in the execution of the order when it was received, or in some other respect whereby the interest of the customer was allowed to suffer.

The other general class of cases is where margin on accounts is swept away by a sudden decline and the broker faces the question whether it is better to sell his customer's stock without an order or to endeavor to carry the customer through the decline with the expectation that the loss, if there is a loss, will be made good by the customer.

The tendency of decisions in these cases is toward holding the broker to rather close ac-

countability for his actions. The point has been
made that the broker in such a case is acting in
a double capacity. First, as a broker executing
an order for a customer for a commission. Second, as a banker in making a loan to this customer, being protected therein by the security of
money deposited and the possession of the stock
purchased. As a broker, the equity might be one
way, while as a banker it might be exactly opposite.

Generally speaking, a banker has no right to
*sell out a loan without notifying the borrower,
except where there has been a special agreement
permitting such action. This fact leads banks
and institutions in nearly all cases to make loans
with a formal agreement authorizing them to
sell the collateral at their option in case the loan
ceases to be satisfactory. As a matter of practice, banks call for more collateral when prices
decline. But in cases of panic, or the inability
of brokers to furnish more collateral, loans are
frequently sold out, under the special agreement
to that effect.

Some commission houses protect themselves
by a formal agreement with customers similar to
that required by banks. When a customer opens
an account, he signs an agreement authorizing
the broker to sell the stock bought at his dis-

cretion in case the margin runs down to the danger line.

This is undoubtedly a wise method, as it removes all doubt as to the position of each party in the premises. Such agreements are not invariably made because in the competition for business brokers do not like to impose restrictions which are not universal and which may have a tendency to drive away custom. Nevertheless, experiences like those of the 9th of May, have a decided tendency toward defining the relations between broker and customer.

The action of the market May 9 was so rapid as to make it impossible for a broker to notify a customer of the need of more margin and get a response in time to be of any use. A 10-point margin was of no use at a time when stocks were falling 10 points in five minutes. There were many cases that day in which wealthy commission houses saw a large percentage of their capital disappear in customers' accounts between 11 and 11:30. The rapidity of the recovery was all that saved multitudes of customers and many commission houses. Loans, small and large, were unsound and sound again before lenders had time to sell even if they had been disposed to do so.

There were, however, many cases where stocks

were sold entailing large losses and the location of these losses is in a number of cases still in legal controversy, with the probability that the decision will turn more or less upon the circumstances peculiar to each case. The 9th of May was a very extraordinary day and allowance must be made for its unusual character. Stock Exchange rules based on the occurrences of the 9th of May would prohibit doing business under ordinary conditions, but such days come and on this account brokers and customers should make provision for the unexpected by a clear understanding as to what shall be done in emergencies.

It is often difficult to say what shall be done when a loss has occurred through unusual conditions and under circumstances which made the action taken largely discretionary. This fact in its application to the May panic has led brokers and customers in cases to adopt a policy of trying to divide the loss equitably and with due reference to the facts involved in that particular case. A jury familiar with Stock Exchange business would be very· likely to render a decision along somewhat similar lines.

CHAPTER XV.

THE RECURRENCES OF CRISES.

A CORRESPONDENT writes: "Is it true that commercial or stock exchange panics are approximately periodic in their occurrence?"

The facts point distinctly in that direction, and there is reason back of the facts. The reason is that the business community has a tendency to go from one extreme to the other. As a whole, it is either contracting business under a belief that prices will be lower or expanding under a belief that prices will be higher. It appears to take ordinarily five or six years for public confidence to go from the point of too little hope to the point of too much confidence and then five or six years more to get back to the condition of hopelessness.

This ten-year movement in England is given in detail by Professor Jevons in his attempt to show that sun spots have some bearing upon commercial affairs. Without going into the matter of sun spots and their bearing upon crops, commerce, or states of minds, it may be assumed that Professor Jevons has stated correctly the periods of depression as they have occurred in England during the last two centuries.

The dates given by him as the years in which commercial crises have occurred follow: 1701, 1711, 1712, 1731-2, 1742, 1752, 1763, 1772-3, 1783, 1804-5, 1815, 1825, 1836, 1847, 1857, 1866 and 1878.

This makes a very good showing for the ten-year theory, and it is supported to a considerable extent by what has occurred in this country during the past century.

The first crisis in the United States during the nineteenth century came in 1814, and was precipitated by the capture of Washington by the British on the 24th of August in that year. The Philadelphia and New York banks suspended payments, and for a time the crisis was acute. The difficulties leading up to this period were the great falling off in foreign trade caused by the embargo and non-intercourse act of 1808, the excess of public expenditures over public receipts, and the creation of a large number of state banks taking the place of the old United States bank. Many of these state banks lacked capital and issued currency without sufficient security.

There was a near approach to a crisis in 1819 as the result of a tremendous contraction of bank circulation. The previous increases of bank issues had promoted speculation, the contraction caused a serious fall in the prices of commodities and real estate. This, however, was purely a money panic as far as its causes were concerned.

The European crisis in 1825 caused a diminished demand for American products and led to lower prices and some money stringency in 1826. The situation, however, did not become very serious and was more in the nature of an interruption to progress than a reversal of conditions.

The year 1837 brought a great commercial panic, for which there was 'abundant cause. There had been rapid industrial and commercial growth, with a multitude of enterprises established ahead of the time. Crops were deficient, and breadstuffs were imported. The refusal of the government to extend the charter of the United States Bank had caused a radical change in the banking business of the country, while the withdrawal of public deposits and their lodgment with state banks had given the foundation for abnormal speculation.

The panic in Europe in 1847 exerted but little influence in this country, although there was a serious loss in specie, and the Mexican war had some effect in checking enterprises. These effects, however, were neutralized somewhat by large exports of breadstuffs and later by the discovery of gold in 1848-9.

There was a panic of the first magnitude in 1857, following the failure of the Ohio Life Insurance & Trust Company in August. This panic came unexpectedly, although prices had been falling for some months. There had been very large railroad building, and the proportion of specie held by banks was very small in proportion to their loans and deposits. One of the features of this period was the great number of failures. The banks generally suspended payments in October.

The London panic in 1866 precipitated by the failure of Overend, Gurney & Co., was followed by heavy fall in prices in the Stock Exchange here. In April there had been a corner in Michigan Southern and rampant speculation generally, from which the relapse was rather more than normal.

The panic of September, 1873, was a commercial as well as a Stock Exchange panic. It was the outcome of an enormous conversion of floating into fixed capital. Business had been expanded on an enormous scale, and the supply of money became insufficient for the demands made upon it. Credit collapsed and the depression was extremely serious.

The year 1884 brought a Stock Exchange smash but not a commercial crisis. The failure of the Marine Bank, Metropolitan Bank and Grant & Ward in May was accompanied by a large fall in prices and a general check which was felt throughout the year. The Trunk Line war, which had lasted for several years, was one of the factors in this period.

The panic of 1893 was the outcome of a number of causes—uncertainty in regard to the currency situation, the withdrawal of foreign investments and the fear of radical tariff legislation. The anxiety in regard to the maintenance of the gold standard was undoubtedly the chief factor, as it bore upon many others.

Judging by the past and by the developments of the last six years, it is not unreasonable to suppose that we may get at least a stock exchange flurry in the next few years. This decade seems to be the one for the small crisis instead of the large one—a type of 1884 rather than a recurrence of 1837, 1873 or 1893. (*See Note* 13.)

NOTE 13.—Mr. Dow's forecast here was verified by the "undigested securities" panic of 1903, which was confined almost entirely to investments, business in general suffering but little. Later panics came in 1907 and 1914.